TIME FOR KIDS

X WHY Z

YOUR BODY

By Mark Shulman and James Buckley Jr.

TIME FOR KIDS
Managing Editor, TIME FOR KIDS Magazine: Nellie Gonzalez Cutler
Creative Director: Jennifer Kraemer-Smith
Project Editor: Vickie An

Publisher Margot Schupf
Vice President, Finance Vandana Patel
Executive Director, Marketing Services Carol Pittard
Executive Director, Business Development Suzanne Albert
Executive Director, Marketing Susan Hettleman
Executive Publishing Director Megan Pearlman
Associate Director of Publicity Courtney Greenhalgh
Assistant General Counsel Simone Procas
Assistant Director, Special Sales Ilene Schreider
Assistant Director, Finance Christine Font
Assistant Production Director Susan Chodakiewicz
Senior Manager, Sales Marketing Danielle Costa
Senior Manager, Children's Category Marketing Amanda Lipnick
Manager, Business Development and Partnerships Stephanie Braga
Associate Production Manager Amy Mangus
Associate Prepress Manager Alex Voznesenskiy

Editorial Director Stephen Koepp
Art Director Gary Stewart
Senior Editors Roe D'Angelo, Alyssa Smith
Managing Editor Matt DeMazza
Editor, Children's Books Jonathan White
Copy Chief Rina Bander
Design Manager Anne-Michelle Gallero
Assistant Managing Editor Gina Scauzillo
Editorial Assistant Courtney Mifsud

Created at Oomf, Inc.
www.Oomf.com

By Mark Shulman and James Buckley Jr.
Designed by Bill Madrid
Educational Consultant: Kara Pranikoff

Special thanks: Alysson Angle, Keith Aurelio, Katherine Barnet, Brad Beatson, Jeremy Biloon, Ian Chin, Lena Cigleris, Rose Cirrincione, Pat Datta, Assu Etsubneh, Alison Foster, Kristina Jutzi, David Kahn, Jean Kennedy, Hillary Leary, Samantha Long, Kimberly Marshall, Robert Martells, Nina Mistry, Mark Orenshein, Kevin Pranikoff, Melissa Presti, Danielle Prielipp, Kate Roncinske, Babette Ross, Dave Rozzelle, Matthew Ryan, Ricardo Santiago, Divyam Shrivastava, Gabriel Zatlin

For information on TIME FOR KIDS magazine for the
classroom or home, go to TIMEFORKIDS.COM
or call 1-800-777-8600.
For subscriptions to SI KIDS, go to
SIKIDS.COM or call 1-800-889-6007.

Published by TIME FOR KIDS Books,
An imprint of Time Inc. Books
1271 Avenue of the Americas, 6th Floor
New York, NY 10020

ISBN 10: 1-61893-137-7
ISBN 13: 978-1-61893-137-5
Library of Congress Control Number: 2015934817

TIME FOR KIDS is a trademark of Time Inc.

We welcome your comments and suggestions about TIME FOR KIDS Books. Please write to us at:
TIME FOR KIDS Books, Attention: Book Editors, P.O. Box 361095, Des Moines, IA 50336-1095
If you would like to order any of our hardcover Collector's Edition books, please call us at 1-800-327-6388 (Monday through Friday,
7 a.m. to 8 p.m., Central Time).
1 QGT 15

TIME FOR KIDS
X WHY Z YOUR BODY

CONTENTS

WELCOME!

WHY IS MY BODY SO INCREDIBLE?

You are amazing, and so is your body.

This book answers many questions you may ask about all the incredible things your body can do.

On every page, your brain will learn something new!

Remember to look for the **WHY? FACT:** boxes to find out even more.

You'll grow very smart!

WHY IS MY BODY BETTER THAN A MACHINE?

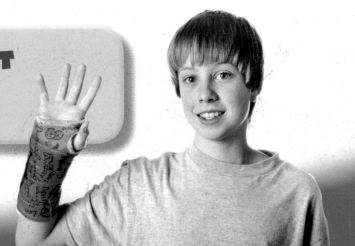

WHEN IT WANTS TO DO SOMETHING
…it teaches itself.

WHEN IT NEEDS ENERGY
…it finds fuel.

AND WHEN IT GETS HURT
…it even fixes itself!

MUSCLES & BONES

Your bones give your body its shape.

Your muscles move you and your bones around in the world!

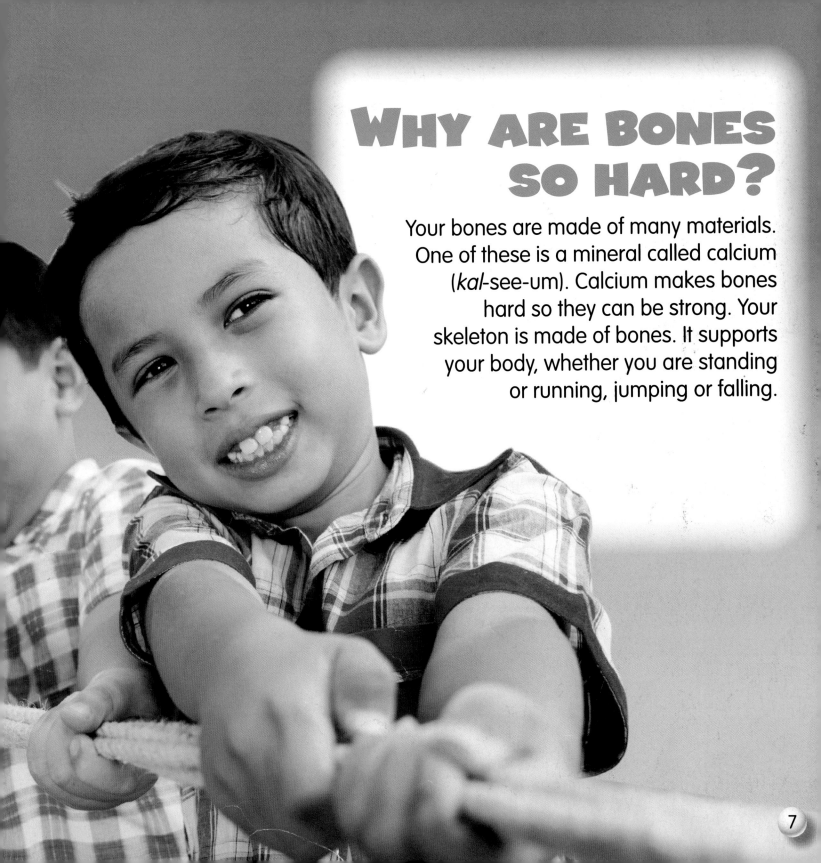

WHY ARE BONES SO HARD?

Your bones are made of many materials. One of these is a mineral called calcium (*kal*-see-um). Calcium makes bones hard so they can be strong. Your skeleton is made of bones. It supports your body, whether you are standing or running, jumping or falling.

WHY DO I HAVE BIG TOES?

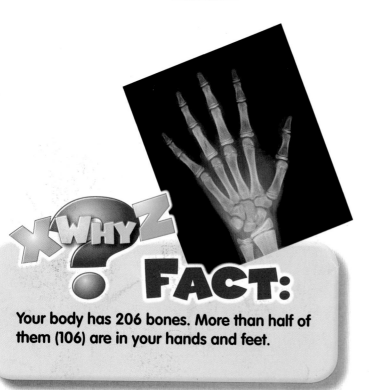

Your big toes are there to help you balance. They give your foot an extra push off the ground when you walk or run. They also help keep you from falling over.

Test yourself! Stand up and lift your toes. Now put your toes down. Do you feel the difference?

XWHYZ FACT:

Your body has 206 bones. More than half of them (106) are in your hands and feet.

WHY ARE MY THUMBS SO SPECIAL?

Humans are the only animals with thumbs that can reach all the way across their hands. Try picking something up without using your thumb. It's hard! Having thumbs helps you get a good grip on stuff. This includes all of the tools we use to build things.

MUSCLES & BONES

WHY DO MY KNEES BEND?

Your knees bend because they are joints. If your knees didn't bend, you'd have a hard time getting around. Your knee connects the bones in your upper and lower leg. Flexible cords called tendons attach your knee bones to your leg muscles.

Try walking across the room without bending your knees. It's not easy!

XWHYZ FACT:

The bottom halves of your arms and legs have two main bones each. The top half of each of your arms and legs has one main bone.

XWHYZ? FACT:

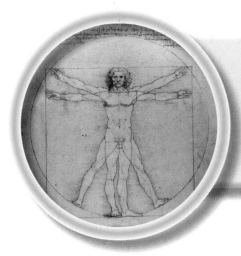

Stretch your arms out wide. The distance between your fingertips is about the same as your height. That is what this famous picture by artist Leonardo da Vinci is showing.

WHY DOES MY FOOT HAVE AN ARCH?

The arch in your foot makes it easier for you to stand and walk. The arch works like a spring. It gives each footstep more bounce. This is more comfortable for your legs and feet, which carry all your weight. Some people have arches that are lower than usual. They have flat feet.

Look at your feet. Do you have a high arch or a low arch?

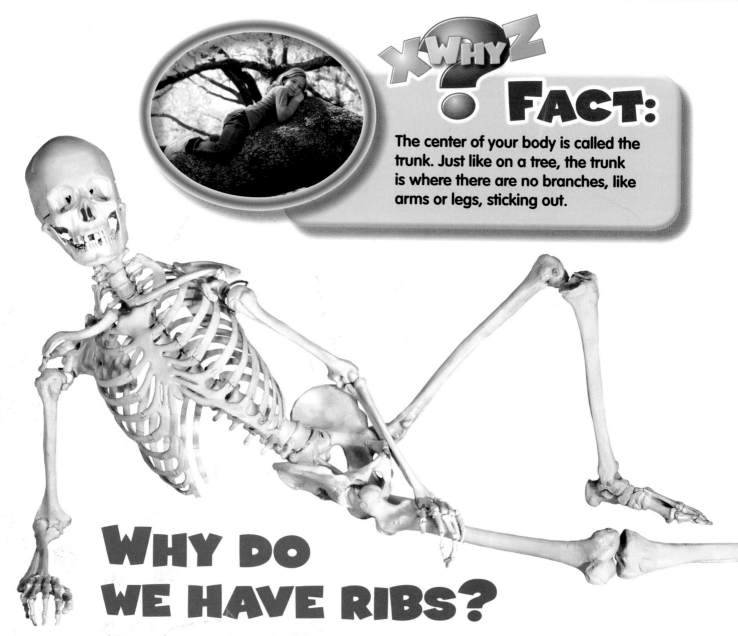

The center of your body is called the trunk. Just like on a tree, the trunk is where there are no branches, like arms or legs, sticking out.

WHY DO WE HAVE RIBS?

Ribs are bones that protect the organs in the center of your body. Your ribs work like a cage. They hold your heart and lungs, two of your body's most important organs.

Why do some belly buttons look different?

Did you know that your belly button is a scar? Before babies are born, they are connected to their mom by a tube. The tube is cut right after birth. It leaves a small hole. When the hole heals, we call the leftover scar a belly button. If there is extra skin, the belly button sticks out. That's an outie!

Does your belly button stick in or out?

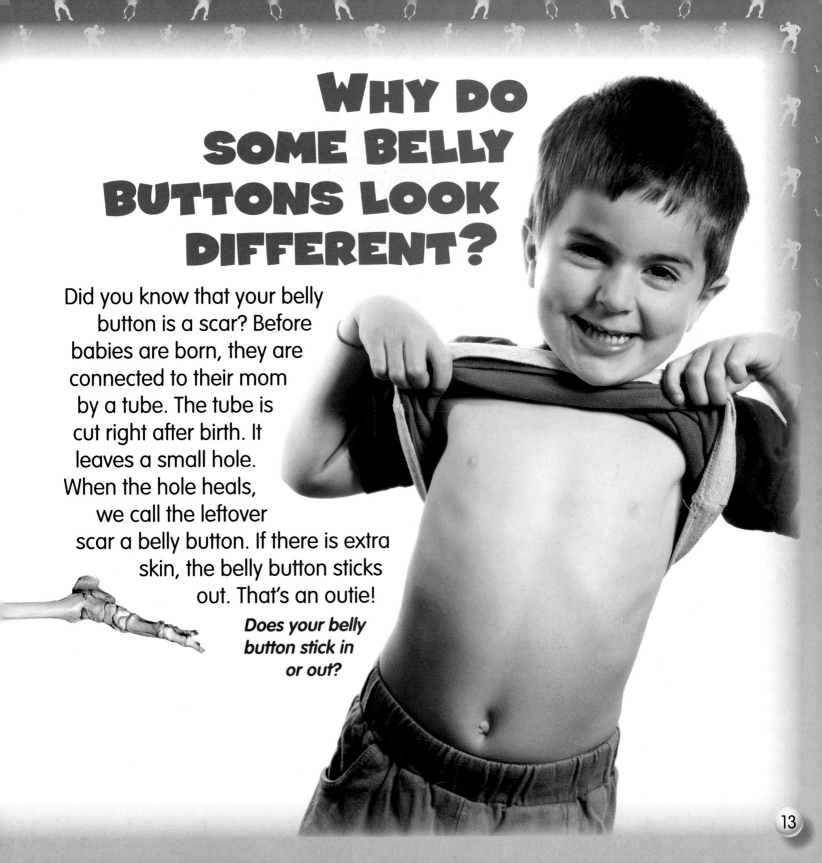

WHY IS MY SKULL SO HARD?

Your skull is made of 22 bones. The bones fit together to form a strong, hard case. It protects your brain, which is the most important part of your body. The skull helps keep your brain in your head, where it belongs.

FACT:

Your ears have bones, and they are all on the inside of your head.

WHY IS MY BACKBONE ABLE TO BEND?

Your backbone is flexible because it is made of separate pieces of bone. These pieces are called vertebrae (*ver*-tuh-bray). They link together to make a sort of chain. If your backbone were one long, hard bone, you could not bend over to tie your shoes!

FACT:

When babies are born, all the pieces of their skull usually haven't joined together yet. Until those parts connect, the soft spots between them are called fontanelles (fon-tah-*nells*).

X WHY Z FACT:

People with dental problems sometimes have to wear false teeth. These teeth are called dentures.

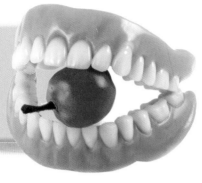

WHY DO I GET CAVITIES?

Food that sticks to your teeth can turn into stuff called plaque (*plack*). Plaque can eat through the hard enamel (ee-*nam*-uhl) of your teeth and cause holes, or cavities. Keep brushing your teeth to brush away that plaque. And don't forget to floss!

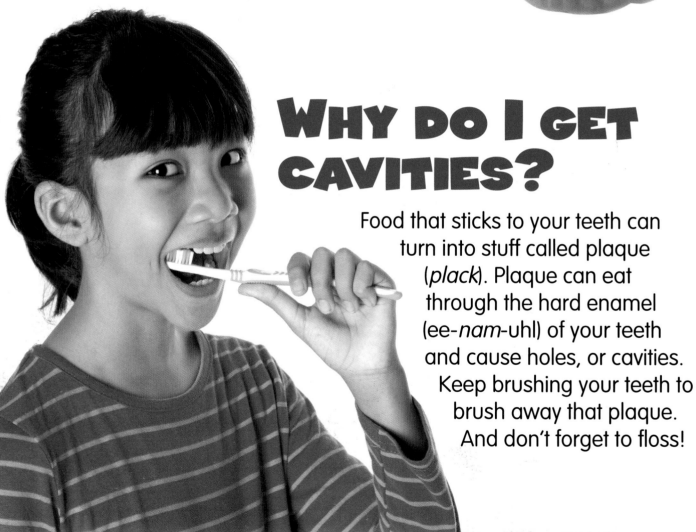

WHY DO MY TEETH FALL OUT?

We are all born with two sets of teeth. Your baby teeth grow in first. When you turn 6 or 7, your jaw grows to its adult size. This is when your adult teeth start pushing up, and your baby teeth fall out.

FACT:

Why are some teeth flat and some pointed? Flat teeth help you grind your food so it can be swallowed. Sharper teeth are used to cut, tear and bite harder foods.

WHY AM I COVERED IN MUSCLES?

Muscles are the meat connected to your bones. You have more than 650 muscles in your body. Their main job is to help you move. Muscles give you the strength to stand up or sit down. As you use your muscles, they release energy. This helps your body stay warm.

XWHYZ FACT:

Stretchy cords called ligaments (*lig*-ah-mints) connect your bones to each other. Other cords called tendons connect muscles to bones.

WHY DO MUSCLES GET BIGGER WHEN THEY'RE STRONG?

When you lift things, jump or run around, you are exercising your muscles. Every time you use a muscle, blood flows to it. The more you exercise, the more blood the muscle has to store. Over time, your muscle gets larger to store that extra blood . . . and you get big, strong muscles!

WHY CAN I MAKE MY VOICE LOUDER AND SOFTER?

You have muscles in your throat called vocal cords. They move together and vibrate when you speak, using air from your lungs. Your vocal cords help control the volume of your voice. When there's more air and more vibration, you are yelling. When you use very little air with gentle vibrations, you're whispering.

WHY IS MY TONGUE SO FLEXIBLE?

Can you roll your tongue, flip it or curl it up and down? Your little tongue has eight different muscles that allow it to move all around your mouth.

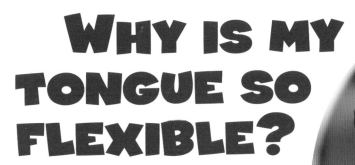

X WHY Z ? FACT:

You have one muscle that is not connected to a bone. It's your heart. No bones about it!

BODY SYSTEMS

When different parts work together, that's called a system.

Your body is filled with systems!

Systems help you breathe, eat, move your blood and more!

Each body system has an important job to do.

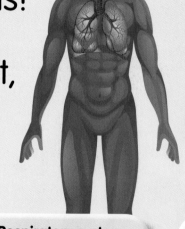

Respiratory system (breathing)

Skeletal system (bones)

WHY DO BODY SYSTEMS WORK TOGETHER?

All the systems of the body have to work together to help you live. The blood system needs air, so it has to work with the breathing system. The food system needs blood to digest (die-*jest*) a meal, so it works with the blood system. And all this happens without you having to think about it!

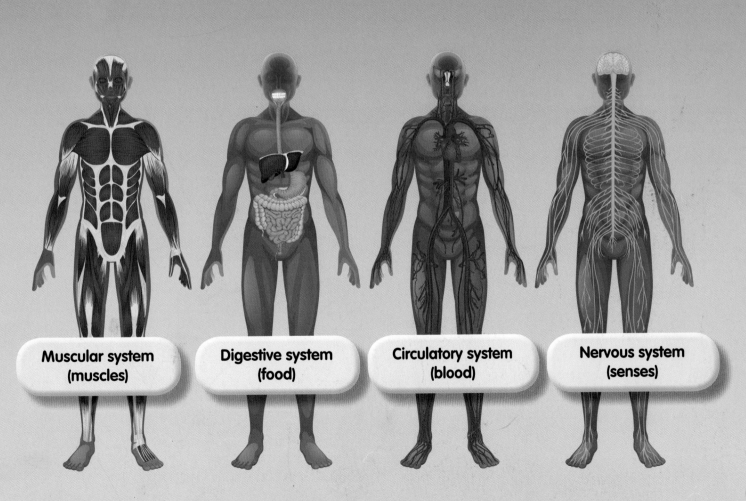

Muscular system
(muscles)

Digestive system
(food)

Circulatory system
(blood)

Nervous system
(senses)

BODY SYSTEMS

WHY DOES BLOOD MOVE THROUGH MY BODY?

Your blood is the delivery system for many things in your body. Blood carries oxygen and food everywhere inside you. It helps deliver messages from your brain. It removes waste from your body parts, too. Your heart pumps the blood around and around many times a minute, so everything stays healthy.

X WHY Z ? FACT:

Those blue lines on your wrist are veins (*vaynz*). They carry blood. But blood is not blue. Veins are not blue, either. The light makes them look blue under your skin. Blood is always red.

WHY CAN PEOPLE DONATE BLOOD TO OTHERS?

You have one of four different types of blood: A, B, AB or O. Sometimes when a person gets sick, he or she needs fresh blood. People who have the same blood type can share their blood. Healthy adults can choose to donate their blood every few months to help other people.

X WHY Z FACT:

Your body has miles and miles of tubes called blood vessels that carry blood. Arteries (*ar*-tur-eez) carry fresh blood away from the heart and lungs. This blood is filled with the oxygen we breathe and other good things for the body. Veins bring blood back to the heart to get refreshed.

WHY CAN I FEEL MY HEARTBEAT IN MY WRIST?

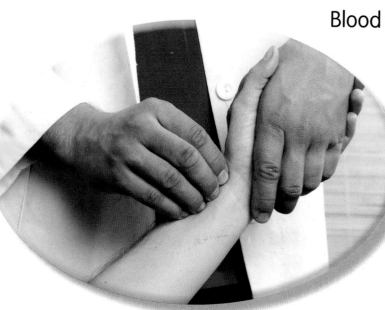

Blood vessels in your wrist are very close to the skin. This makes it easier to feel the blood from your heart pumping through them. The light throbbing you feel is called a pulse. It can be felt in many parts of your body. But the wrist is very handy!

Press down on your wrist. Does your pulse feel fast or slow?

FACT:

Your heart is made of four key parts: two atriums (*ay*-tree-umz) and two ventricles (*ven*-trih-kuls). Each are little empty places, called chambers, that fill and empty with blood over and over!

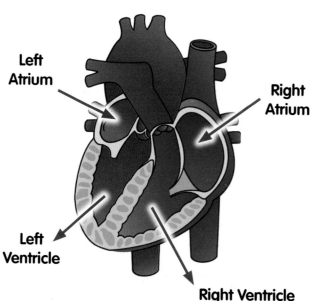

Left Atrium

Right Atrium

Left Ventricle

Right Ventricle

WHY DOES MY HEART POUND WHEN I RUN?

Your muscles need blood to work. And when they work harder, they need even more blood. Your heart pumps blood faster when you run or play. It also beats faster when you're scared. Why? Because your body is getting your muscles ready so you can run away!

FACT:

When something you drink goes into your lungs by mistake, you cough to keep that stuff out. We say it went down the wrong way. It sure did!

WHY DO I BREATHE?

You breathe because your body needs oxygen. Oxygen is the invisible gas that surrounds us in the air. Oxygen helps us turn food into energy. When you breathe air into your lungs, your blood carries the oxygen to every part of your body. You breathe every few seconds for your whole life. Now take a deep breath!

WHY DOES MY CHEST MOVE WHEN I BREATHE?

Inside your chest are your lungs. They are like balloons. Each time you inhale, or breathe in, you fill your lungs with air. This makes your lungs get larger. When you exhale, or breathe out, the air leaves your lungs, and they get smaller again.

FACT:

Your mouth and your nose are both connected to your windpipe. Your windpipe is your trachea (*tray*-kee-uh). It brings air to your lungs.

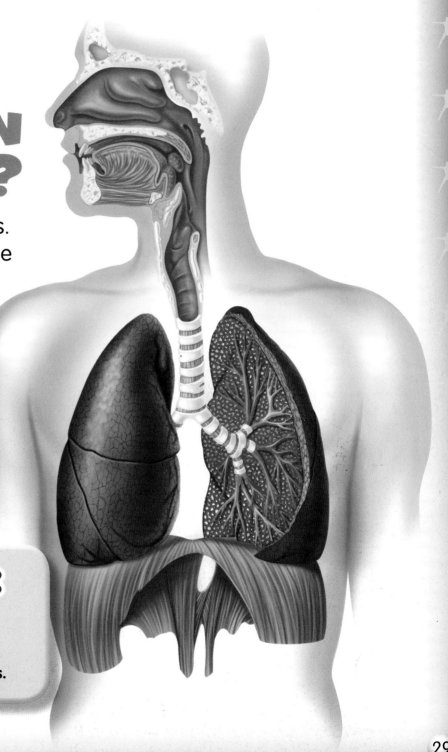

WHY CAN I SEE MY BREATH WHEN IT'S COLD?

Your body is always warm! It's as hot as a summer day. The breath inside you is just as warm as your body. When the wet, hot air from your lungs meets the dry, cold air outside, it forms a little cloud.

X WHY Z ? FACT:

Next time you see a tree or a plant, hug it and say thanks! Plants make some of the oxygen we need to live.

WHY CAN'T I HOLD MY BREATH FOR A LONG TIME?

You need to breathe all day and all night to bring oxygen into your body. You could not live even a few minutes without oxygen. Holding your breath for a long time is not good for you. Don't even try!

WHY DO I GET HUNGRY?

Food is the main fuel for your body. Food gives you energy, and it helps your body grow and stay healthy. Your body burns food like a fire burns logs. When your body uses up the food you've eaten, it lets you know it needs more by feeling hungry. The more energy you burn, the more you need to eat.

WHY IS SPIT SO IMPORTANT?

The real name for spit is saliva (suh-*lie*-vuh). Its job is to help break down food as you chew and make it easier to swallow. Saliva helps keep your teeth clean. And sometimes it helps you fight bad breath.

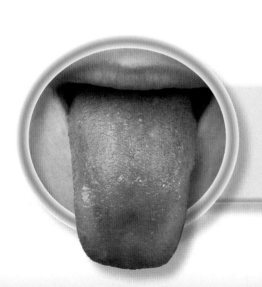

X WHY Z FACT:

Those bumps on the top of your tongue are for tasting food. They're called taste buds.

WHY DO I FART?

There are bacteria inside you that help break down the food in your body. When these bacteria gobble up the food you eat, they make gas. The gas fills up inside you, and it needs to come out. So your body releases gas in that famous loud and smelly way. It's natural, but it can sound pretty rude!

WHY DO I PEE?

Your body only keeps a part of what you eat and drink. The food it doesn't need has to go. And that's when *you* have to go . . . to the bathroom. Pee is the liquid (*lik*-wid) that your body wants to get rid of. It stores in your bladder until you feel ready to flush it away.

WHY DO I POOP?

The leftover solid food you eat is stored in a part of your body called the large intestine (in-*tess*-tin). When enough unwanted food is built up in the intestine, it pushes through like toothpaste out of a tube. Out it goes!

XWHYZ FACT:

Poop smells bad to you. But it smells good to bugs and other creatures. It also helps plants grow.

WHY ARE TWO EARS BETTER THAN ONE?

FACT:

Dogs have amazing ears. They can hear very high sounds that humans can't. A dog whistle doesn't sound like anything to us. But to a dog, the whistle sounds really loud.

Two ears make your hearing better. You can hear a voice from 10 feet away using one ear. But you'll hear the same voice from 40 feet away using both ears. Having two ears also helps your brain know where a sound is coming from.

WHY DO I GET WAX IN MY EARS?

Earwax is the sticky stuff our ears make. It traps and collects things from the air that might damage your delicate ear bones. Think of this wax as boogers for the ear.

WHY CAN BAD SMELLS BE A GOOD THING?

Our sense of smell has evolved over millions of years to help us sniff out danger. Bad smells stop us from eating bad food. The smell of smoke warns us of fire. And a cave that smelled like a bear would have given this warning to a caveman: "Don't go in there!"

WHY DO I HAVE EYEBROWS AND EYELASHES?

Eyebrows and eyelashes protect your eyes. Your eyebrows keep sweat from rolling into your eyes, and protect them from the sun. Your eyelashes trap dust and other small particles before they enter your eyes. Neither of them will keep fingers out of your eyes, so be careful!

X WHY Z FACT:

If you cross your eyes, they will not stay that way. But it won't help either.

WHY CAN I SEE BETTER WHEN I SQUINT?

When you squint, you are squeezing and changing the shape of your eye. Like a camera, your eye has a lens. And like a camera, you can shift your lens to see more clearly. You may look funny, but you'll see a bit better!

Do you squint a lot? You might need glasses!

WHY DO ADULTS HAVE DEEPER VOICES THAN KIDS?

In boys especially, a part of the throat called the larynx (*lare*-inks) gets bigger during the teenage years. The vocal cords that control sound get thicker and longer too. Together, that creates a deeper tone to the adult voice.

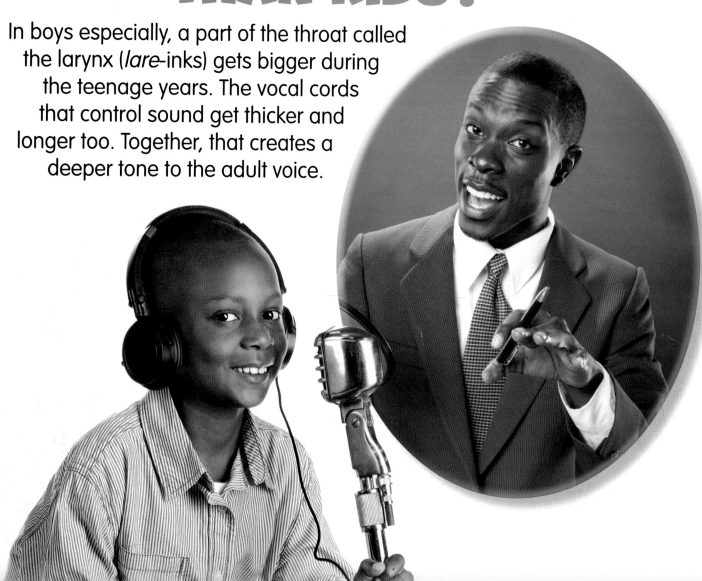

WHY DO BABIES CRY?

Crying is a way for babies to tell you something. Since they can't talk, they cry to show they're hungry or upset.

X WHY Z FACT:

Scientists have lots of guesses, but no one knows for sure why people yawn.

WHY ARE FINGERPRINTS HELPFUL?

Fingerprints are the swirly lines on the tips of your fingers. No two people have the exact same fingerprints. When the police find fingerprint marks at a crime scene, it helps them figure out who was there.

X WHY Z ? FACT:

Toes and fingers that have been soaking in water can look like raisins. That's because skin can soak up water like a sponge.

WHY DO I GET GOOSEBUMPS?

Goosebumps can appear on your skin when you feel cold or scared. This is because your body is covered in tiny hairs. The hairs naturally stand up when you get chilly or feel afraid. They pull on the skin around them, raising little bumps.

WHY DO I SWEAT?

Sweat is your body's way of cooling off when it gets too hot. It also carries away some of the chemicals your body doesn't want anymore. We have between two million and four million tiny glands that let out sweat through the skin.

FACT:

The color of your hair depends on the color of your parents' hair. If your hair is a different color than theirs, someone else in your family had that hair color.

WHY DO SOME PEOPLE HAVE CURLY HAIR?

People can have two different types of hair. Their hair can be rounded like a tube, or flatter like a dry noodle. If the hairs are flatter, they will be curly. If they are rounded, they'll grow straight. Your parents' hair will usually decide what kind of hair you end up with.

Do you have curly or straight hair? What about your mom or dad?

WHY DOESN'T ARM HAIR GROW VERY LONG?

Hair on your arms does not grow all the time. It stops and takes a rest every few months. After the hair rests, the old arm hair falls out and new arm hair grows. That's why arm hair doesn't grow very long. The hair on your head spends much more time growing, so it gets a lot longer.

WHY DO SOME MEN GO BALD?

Many men who go bald can thank their fathers or grandfathers. If a man loses his hair later in his life, his sons probably will also. Men have genes that cause the hair to fall out in a pattern. Some women lose hair in the same way.

45

WHY DOES FOOD GIVE ME ENERGY?

Food is our most important source of energy. Everything you eat—fruits, vegetables or animals—used energy to grow. Once you eat that food, you get the food's energy inside you. Your body will use many chemicals that are in the food you eat. Those chemicals give your body energy.

WHY DO I NEED TO EAT FRESH FOOD?

Fresh foods provide the most valuable kinds of energy and chemicals that your body needs. When you make healthy food choices, you help your body work right. Eating only pasta every night won't give your body the vitamins and minerals that are only found in plants. If you want to be strong and healthy, eat fresh foods.

WHY DO I GET THIRSTY?

Your body is made mostly of water. When you feel thirsty, your body is telling you that you don't have enough water. You can live much longer without food than you can without water. Be sure to drink enough!

WHY DO I LIKE EATING THE SAME FOOD OVER AND OVER?

When you always want a certain food, there is a reason. Sometimes the food makes you feel happy. Sometimes it's because someone always makes it for you. Sometimes your body is telling you what it likes. Everyone has different tastes. But remember, your body needs different kinds of foods to stay healthy.

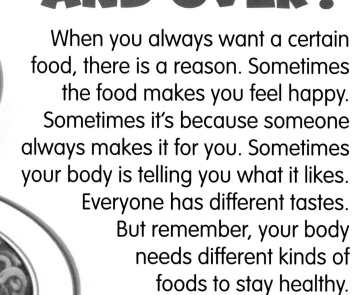

WHY DO I LIKE DIFFERENT FOODS THAN OTHER PEOPLE IN MY FAMILY?

Just because you are related to someone doesn't mean you are exactly the same. Every person's tongue tastes foods in different ways. Tell that to your parents when they serve you *their* favorite vegetable!

X WHY Z

? FACT:

Different foods grow in different parts of the globe. Exploring the world of food is a great way to travel . . . without leaving home!

WHY DO WE EAT SWEET FOOD?

When you are feeling tired, there is less sugar in your blood to give you energy. Sweet, sugary foods such as cookies, candy and soda raise your blood sugar levels right away to give you a boost. But this sugar is actually an empty food. It doesn't help your body at all. Pretty soon you will crash, get tired again, and your body will want more junk food! Enjoy a taste, but not too much.

WHY DO WE EAT SALTY SNACKS?

Salt is a chemical that's already in your body. When you are active, you lose some of that salt in your sweat. So your body wants to eat more. However, it is hard for your body to know when to stop. Salty snacks can taste good. But too much salt is bad for your body, so be careful.

X WHY Z FACT:

To keep your body strong and healthy, you need to eat a balanced diet. Look at this MyPlate chart. About half of what you eat should be fruits and vegetables. Grains include rice, pasta and bread. Protein includes meat and beans. Dairy products are made of milk. Hey, where are the cookies?

WHY SHOULD I STAY AWAY FROM OLD FOOD?

There is nothing pleasant about old food. It can look bad. It can feel bad. It can smell bad. And it can taste bad. Even worse, old food often has dangerous bacteria growing on it. There might also be insects sharing that old food with you. That's why so many foods have expiration dates!

FACT:

Your hands are covered in dirt and bacteria that can make you sick. You don't want that in your mouth! Wash your hands often to stay healthy.

WHY CAN'T SOME PEOPLE EAT NUTS?

Sometimes a type of food can make some people sick. This means they have an allergy (*al*-er-jee) to that food. Many people are allergic to peanuts and other nuts. Sometimes just the smell of nuts can make those people sick. Many schools have special rules when a student has a nut allergy.

BRAIN & NERVES

Your brain remembers so much.

It also uses your nervous system to explore the world and find out what's good for you and what isn't.

What a smart brain you have!

WHY IS MY BRAIN IN CHARGE OF MY BODY?

Every system needs a boss to help things run well. Your brain is that boss. It controls your breathing and heartbeat. It handles every way you move your body. It collects all the information you get from your five senses. Your brain also helps you create ideas, feelings and dreams. It's a busy place.

BRAIN & NERVES

FACT:

Ever hit your funny bone at your elbow? It's not funny, and it's not really a bone! It's called the ulnar nerve. Banging it gives your arm and hand a strange tingle.

WHY CAN I FEEL THINGS I TOUCH?

Nerves are found under every part of your skin. The nerves sense what you touch and send that message instantly to your brain. Your brain stores memories of how things feel. That's why you can remember if something is smooth or rough, soft or hard.

WHY DOES SPINNING MAKE ME DIZZY?

Your inner ears, inside your head, keep track of where your body is.
When you spin, you confuse those inner ear parts. When you stop spinning,
they think you're still moving for a moment. That's why you feel dizzy!

WHY IS MY BRAIN DIVIDED IN TWO PARTS?

Your brain is divided into left and right halves. That's because each side of the brain is in charge of one side of your body. But each half crosses sides! The left side of the brain controls the right side of your body, and the right side of the brain controls the left side of your body.

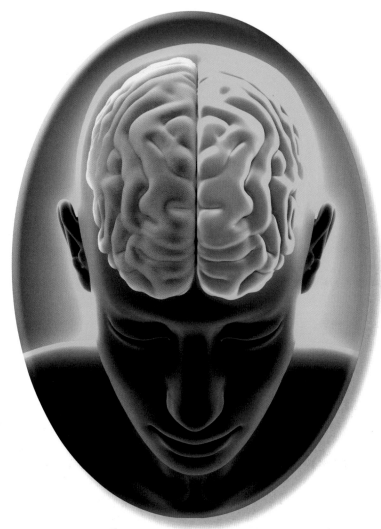

WHY Z FACT:

Believe it or not, your brain feels like tofu!

WHY CAN I REMEMBER THINGS?

Everything you remember is stored in your brain. But your memories are not stored in the same place. Smells, faces, sounds and feelings are all kept in different areas. When you remember something, you are putting all those parts back together again.

Think about what you did yesterday. Which things do you remember?

59

WHY DO I HAVE DIFFERENT SENSES?

Your senses help you gather information from the world around you. Your eyes, ears, nose, mouth and skin tell you different things about whatever you find. Right now, each of your five main senses is telling you something about what you see, hear, smell, taste or feel.

1.
Hearing

2.
Feeling

3. Seeing

5.
Tasting

4.
Smelling

X WHY Z

? FACT:

Please, please, please wear a good helmet when you bike or skateboard. You only have one brain, so you need to protect it.

WHY ARE CONCUSSIONS DANGEROUS?

A concussion (kun-*kuh*-shun) is a type of injury to the brain. It happens when someone gets hit in the head very hard, causing the brain to smack into the skull. Getting more than one concussion can lead to serious problems. When you think about all the things a brain does, you want to keep it safe!

WHY DOES BEING HAPPY GIVE ME ENERGY?

When you are happy, your body makes chemicals. The same thing happens when you exercise too. Those chemicals give you energy and make you feel good. Your body is telling you: "Do that again!"

WHY DO I WANT TO RUN WHEN I'M SCARED?

Early humans lived in a world filled with danger from animals and other humans. They had to learn to escape quickly at the first sign of trouble. Our brains haven't changed that much since then. When something scares us, we jump!

WHY DO I CRY WHEN I'M SAD?

Being sad can cause a lot of unhappy energy to build up inside you. Crying helps release some of that energy. Another reason we may cry is to signal to others that we need help or comfort.

WHY DO I NEED TO SLEEP?

Kids ask this question every night! Sleep helps us get back energy. It lets our minds slow down so our bodies can make important repairs. Sleep is when we do our growing and healing. Kids need about 10 to 12 hours of sleep each night to stay healthy.

Keep a sleep diary! Every day when you wake up, write down how many hours you slept.

X WHY Z ? FACT:

Scientists say that nearly one out of every three people has walked in their sleep at least once!

WHY DO I DREAM?

Dreams are one of the biggest mysteries of science. Some experts say dreams and nightmares help you think about something important in your life. Others think they're messages about the future. No one knows exactly why our brains create dreams.

What was the last thing you dreamed about?

WHY DO SOME PEOPLE SNORE?

Snoring happens when air can't flow smoothly through the throat. People snore for many reasons. One common cause is a clogged nose or another kind of blocked breathing. Different tools have been invented to help stop snoring. But the most effective tools are earplugs—for whoever can hear the snoring!

FEELING SICK

We all need to keep our bodies healthy.

But sometimes we get sick and tired.

Then it's time to get better!

WHY DO GERMS MAKE ME SICK?

Germs are very tiny. But they can make you sick in a big way. Many kinds of germs attack healthy parts of your body. The germs get stronger while you get weaker. Sleep, good food and medicine give you the strength to fight back!

WHY DO I BURP?

First you eat the food. Then your body digests the food, breaking it into smaller and smaller pieces. The bacteria inside you that break down the food make a gas. We also swallow air when we eat and drink. The gas inside you needs to come out somehow.

When it goes up your throat, that's a burp!

WHY DO I COUGH?

Coughing is your body's way of clearing something out of your throat. Coughs can also be caused by dust, allergies or sickness. If you need to cough, block those germs! Cough into the crook of your elbow.

WHY DO I SNEEZE?

Sneezing is a quick, loud way your body gets things out of your nose. Some people also sneeze when they step into the bright sunlight.

FACT:

A sneeze can travel up to 100 miles per hour. That's as fast as a race car!

Can you think of anything else that might make you go "achoo"?

WHY DO I GET BRUISES?

Oops! You bumped into something. Now you have a bruise. That means you're bleeding under your skin, but you're not bleeding outside. It hurts. Soon the bleeding will stop. As it gets better, the color will get darker. Then your bruise goes away.

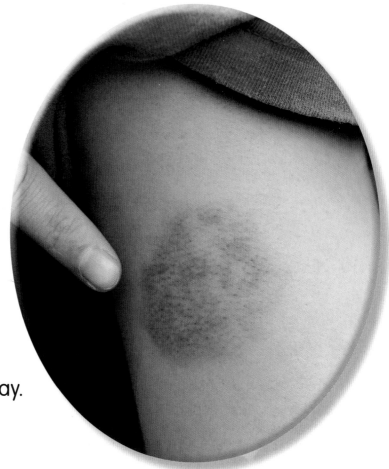

X WHY Z ? FACT:

Washing a cut and keeping it clean keeps out bad germs and bacteria.

WHY DO CUTS TURN INTO SCABS?

When you get a cut, you bleed. Then the blood dries and makes a scab. The hard scab protects your boo-boo while the skin underneath grows back. When the skin is healed, the scab will flake off.

WHY DO I GET BLISTERS?

Blisters can form when your skin rubs against something the wrong way. Sometimes you will see a bubble rise up. It's made by fluid that protects your skin as it heals.

WHY DO BEE STINGS MAKE MY SKIN PUFFY?

When a bee stings . . . ouch! The stinger shoots a tiny bit of venom into you. Your body works to fight off this poison by sending blood cells and other chemicals to the spot. All that in one place causes the skin to swell up.

X WHY Z ? FACT:

If you step on a rusty nail, you might get dirt in the cut. Bacteria in the dirt can cause an illness called tetanus (*teh*-tuh-nuss). Doctors will give you a shot to keep you from getting sick.

WHY CAN THE SUN BURN ME?

Even though it is 93 million miles away, the sun is so hot it can burn your skin. To keep the sun's rays from hurting you, cover up with hats and clothes. You should also wear plenty of sunscreen. Getting sunburned too often can make you sick and harm your skin.

X WHY Z FACT:

Sunscreen does not age well. If you have some that is more than three years old (check the date on the bottle), it won't do the job of protecting you. Toss it!

WHY CAN A FEVER BE GOOD NEWS?

Fevers don't feel good. But they can be good for your body. When you are ill, extra body heat helps you fight or even kill whatever is making you sick. When the fever is gone, it means you're getting better. Then you cool down!

Ask someone to take your temperature today! If you're healthy, your temperature will be around 98.6° F.

WHY IS IT GOOD TO THROW UP SOMETIMES?

When you've swallowed bad food or something your body doesn't want, up it comes. That's good, because keeping the bad stuff inside is even worse than throwing up.

FACT:

Not all germs are bad for you. Some are tiny bacteria that live in your body to help you digest food.

WHY DO I GET MY BLOOD PRESSURE TAKEN?

Sometimes a doctor or a nurse measures your blood pressure. They are seeing how well your blood is flowing through your body. They will put a cuff around your arm, and it squeezes tight. Checking blood pressure is a fast way to find heart problems.

FACT:

Doctors tell you to say "ahh" because your throat opens up wider when you make that sound. That lets doctors get a clearer view of what they want to see down there.

WHY DO DOCTORS AND NURSES LISTEN TO MY HEART?

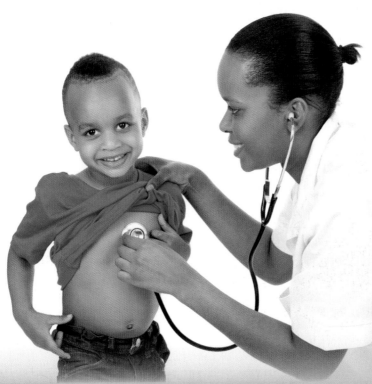

Doctors and nurses can hear more than just your heart beating. They can actually hear parts of the heart open and close as blood moves through. They can hear blood moving too. They know what a healthy heart should sound like. If the doctors hear something that doesn't sound healthy, they can get to work.

WHY DO I SOMETIMES HAVE TO GET A SHOT?

Medicine needs to get into your blood to work. Of all the ways to take medicine, a shot is the fastest. It goes directly into your blood. It only hurts for a moment, and it's better than being sick!

xWHYz FACT:

When you're sick, your body needs good foods to get stronger. Liquids are easier to eat than solid food. Hot steam can help you breathe better. So the next time you're feeling under the weather, have some hot soup!

WHY ARE THERE SO MANY KINDS OF MEDICINE?

Different medicines are made to treat different illnesses. Sometimes there are many kinds of medicines for the same illness. But all medicines have the same job. They give your body the chemicals it needs to fight whatever's wrong. Not all medicine needs to be delivered in a shot. Medicine can also be swallowed. It can be rubbed on like ointment. It can even be breathed in as a gas.

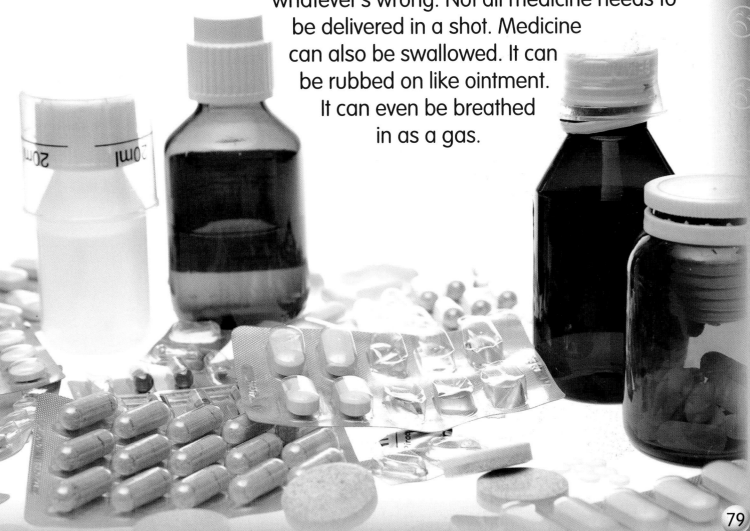

XWHYZ FACT:

This nurse is wearing special hospital clothes called scrubs. Scrubs are cleaner than regular street clothes, which can carry dirt or germs.

WHY DO PEOPLE GO TO THE HOSPITAL?

Most people who are sick or injured can get help at home or at a doctor's office. But for bigger health problems, you need the medical people, machines and medicine found in a hospital. Hospitals care for patients around the clock.

WHY DO SOME SICK PEOPLE RIDE IN AN AMBULANCE?

Getting help fast is important if a person is seriously injured or ill. The back of an ambulance is like a mini-emergency room. Experts can start treating the patient right away. Ambulances can cut through traffic to save time too. They use lights and a siren to say, "Get out of the way!"

WHY DO DOCTORS AND NURSES WEAR MASKS?

A sick person who coughs or sneezes can spread harmful germs. Doctors and nurses wear face masks to keep those germs away.

DIFFERENCES

People may seem different on the outside.

But we are all similar on the inside.

And that's what matters!

WHY DO PEOPLE HAVE DIFFERENT SKIN COLORS?

Your skin color depends on where your ancestors lived thousands of years ago. People who lived in hot, sunny places had darker skin to protect them from the sun's rays. And having lighter skin helped people get more sunlight in less sunny places.

DIFFERENCES

WHY DO SOME PEOPLE GET NEW ARMS OR LEGS?

If a person loses an arm or leg, it is possible to get a new one. These new body parts are made specially to fit the person in need. The parts can move and react much like the real thing!

WHY DO SOME PEOPLE NEED A WHEELCHAIR?

Some people's legs are not strong enough to walk. A wheelchair can help them travel around. A person who breaks a leg may use a wheelchair for a short time. Other people will always need a wheelchair. Some wheelchairs have motors that let the person move with the touch of a button.

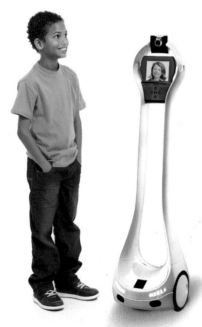

XWHYZ? FACT:

Robots and computers are helping some people see, hear, speak and move, sometimes for the first time.

DIFFERENCES

WHY DO BLIND PEOPLE USE A CANE?

People who are blind can't see. They use a cane to feel the ground in front of them. They are feeling for things they already know. They are also feeling for things that might be in their way. It is a very helpful tool.

WHY DO BLIND PEOPLE USE BRAILLE TO READ?

Braille is an alphabet that uses raised dots to make letters and spell words. Blind people run their fingers across the dots to read the words on the page.

Eat

Drink

More

Please

Thank you

Sorry

WHY DO DEAF PEOPLE TALK WITH THEIR HANDS?

People who are deaf can't hear. They use sign language to communicate. Sign language uses hand movements that spell out words or phrases. A person who knows sign language can understand these movements, just as you understand spoken words.

WHY CAN DOGS HELP PEOPLE WHO ARE BLIND?

Dogs can be trained to act as eyes for the blind. A guide dog goes to school for a long time. When the dog is ready to work, it walks next to a person to warn of objects, curbs or danger. Guide dogs can go to many places that other dogs cannot.

WHY DO DOGS VISIT PEOPLE IN HOSPITALS?

Trained, gentle animals make people happy. Helpers bring these dogs to the hospital to cheer up patients. Doctors say that petting a friendly animal can help people heal faster.

FACT:

Dogs are not the only trained animals that can brighten up a patient's day. Cats, monkeys, rabbits and even llamas do this job too.

DIFFERENCES

WHY DO SOME TWINS LOOK ALIKE?

When the egg in a mother splits in two, each part of the egg grows into a different human being. Because they are from one egg, these two people will look exactly the same. Sometimes they will even act alike. They are called identical twins.

WHY DO SOME TWINS LOOK DIFFERENT?

Some twins come from two different eggs. They will be born at the same time, but they won't look alike. They are called fraternal (frah-*ter*-null) twins.

Do you know any twins? Are they identical or fraternal?

DIFFERENCES

? FACT:

The parts of your body that tell it how to grow are called genes (*jeenz*). Parents pass genes to their children. Those genes tell the child's body's cells how to grow. Someday, they will also pass genes on to *their* children!

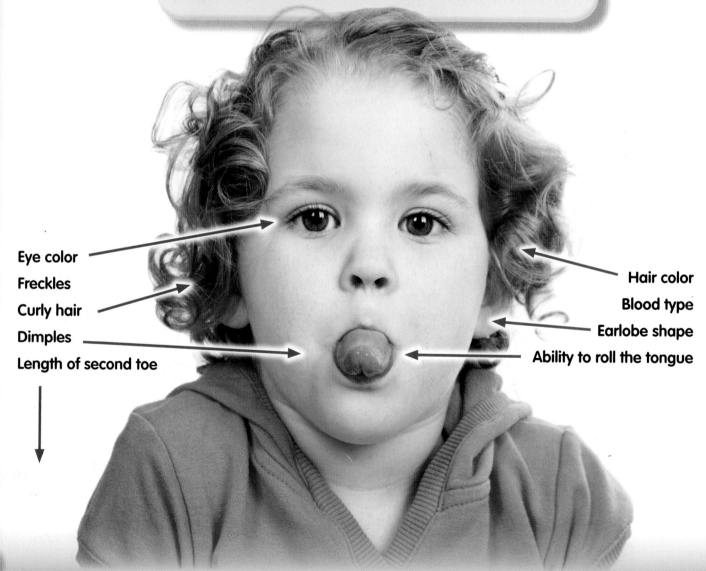

Eye color

Freckles

Curly hair

Dimples

Length of second toe

Hair color

Blood type

Earlobe shape

Ability to roll the tongue

WHY DO I LOOK LIKE MY PARENTS?

There are many things that make you look the way you do. These are called traits (*trates*). Your hair color, your eye color and the shape of your ears are all traits. The picture on the left shows some of the traits that parents pass on to their kids. You probably didn't get all of these traits from your parents, but you got some of them.

What are some of your traits?

GLOSSARY

allergy a bad reaction to something (like a food or a plant) that doesn't bother other people

arteries tubes that carry blood from the heart to the rest of your body

bacteria tiny living organisms, so small they have only one cell each

calcium a mineral that helps make your bones strong

circulatory having to do with moving blood around inside your body

concussion a brain injury caused by a blow to the head

digestive having to do with how food is taken in and used by your body

enamel the hard outer coating of your teeth

esophagus the tube in your throat that moves food to your stomach

genes parts of your DNA that give you traits from your parents

glands cells or organs that help decide which things will be in your blood

larynx a part of your throat that contains your vocal cords

ligaments strong bands of tissue that connect bones to other bones

plaque sticky stuff that builds up on your teeth, eventually eating through the enamel

pulse the repeated beating of your heart

respiratory having to do with parts of your body that help you breathe

saliva the wet stuff in your mouth that helps you break down food

tendons strong bands of tissue that connect muscles to bones

tetanus a disease caused by bacteria that can enter the body when you get cut

trachea the tube in your throat that carries air to and from your lungs

trunk the central part of your body, between your neck and your hips

veins tubes in your body that carry blood to the heart to pick up more oxygen

INDEX